New Word A Day

E S Carruthers

Copyright (c) 2009-2015

Elliot Carruthers

ISBN-13: 978-1492750062

ISBN-10: 1492750069

FORGO (for-goh) abandon; quit; decline.
abstaining from a desired action.
Remember: I FORGOT to GO.
Question: When don't peas appease you?

ASSUAGE (ah-swayge) abate; relieve; soothe.
making something milder or better.
Remember: SWAY and make it better.
Answer: When you don't like peas. Appease means to
calm or pacify

Jan 3

I abridged my book on cats.

ABRIDGE (ah-bridj) abbreviate; truncate; shorten.
condensing something while keeping the idea.
Remember: BRIDGE and combine words.
Question: You have punctilious punctuation. What
should be done to correct it?

Jan 4

We abrogated the contract.

ABROGATE (ab-ro-gate) abolish; reject; nix.
agreeing to an end to something, usually a contract.
Remember: BROS close the GATE between them.
Answer: Nothing. Punctilious means doing
something with care.

BRUSQUE (brusk) abrupt; blunt; curt.
behaving in an unfriendly and direct way.
Remember: BRUSH the wrong way.
Question: You become a sexagenarian. Why can you stay in bed all day?

PILLORIED (pil-lor-reed) abuse; contempt; despise.
ridiculed and punished by a group.
Remember: Punish with a PILLORY.
Answer: You are probably retired. A sexagenarian is at least the age of 60 and younger than 70.

CONTUMELY (kon-toom-lee) abuse; scorn. showing contempt or making an insult.
Remember: CON TO ME.
Question: I say your fame is ephemeral. Why do I talk about fifteen minutes?

AGGRANDIZE (ah-grand-eyes) acclaim; glorify; making it out to be bigger than it is.
Remember: GRAND in our EYES.
Answer: I probably mean the fifteen minutes of fame when someone is famous for a short time.

LAUDATION (law-day-shun) accolade; acclaim; praising someone by giving a speech.
Remember: A LORD before a NATION.
Question: You get comments on the inelegance of your hat. What will you probably do next?

ACCRETION (ah-kre-shun) increment; addition; gradually growing by an outside source.
Remember: ADDITION.
Answer: Stop wearing the hat. Inelegance means ungraceful or crude.

The acrimonious cat was not friendly.

ACRIMONIOUS (ack-kre-moan-ee-us) acrid; bitter.
behaving in a bitter or caustic way.
Remember: ACRID so MOAN US.
Question: What kind of phrase is a banal one?

The obdurate cat would not get off my book.

OBDURATE (ob-jer-rayt) adamant; harsh; dogged;
stubborn and indifferent to advice.
Remember: OBJECT at a fast RATE.
Answer: A banal phrase is a boring saying

The little annex sat next to the big building.

ANNEX (an-neks) addition; attachment; appendix; an extension to an existing building.
Remember: A NEXT
Question: How many utters does a cow have?

Jan 14

EFFICACY (ef-fah-ka-see) effectiveness; potency; producing a positive and strong effect.
Remember: EFFICIENTLY.
Answer: None. Cows can't talk. The meaning of Utter is to talk. Cows have udders.

Jan 15

NIGH (nye) adjacent; bordering; near; close or near.

Remember: So near I SIGH.

Question: You give your cat a quibble and a bowl of pasteurised milk. Why is it not eating?

Jan 16

UPBRAID (up-brayed) admonish; castigate; censure: blaming or scolding.

Remember: UP BRAY when we scold.

Answer: Quibble means to argue. You gave your cat an argument.

Jan 17

QUASI (kwa-zeye) alike; partly; so-called; resembling or being alike.
Remember: QUA to our EYE (Qua means being).
Question: You walk in the woods. You enjoy the preternatural scenery. Why do you feel funny?

Jan 18

ENVENOM (en-ven-nom) anger; enrage; infuriate; angering another with your actions.
Remember: Put IN VENOM and anger.
Answer: Preternatural means being unusual. You feel funny because the scenery is unusual and strange.

Jan 19

ENNUI (on-we) apathy; melancholy; weariness; tired and bored.

Remember: Boredom is ON WE.

Question: We are walking to the dress shop. You trip and I catch you. I say, "You are abreast to me." Why did I say that?

Jan 20

WINSOME (win-sum) appealing; captivating; causing joy or pleasure.

Remember: WIN SOME when we captivate.

Answer: We are walking side-by-side. Abreast means side-by-side.

Jan 21

CODICIL (kod-dis-sil) appendix; postscript;
an addition to a document.
Remember: CO (partner) DICTIONARY.
Question: We are at the zoo and you are lionized.
Your nametag is blank. How do I know who you are?

Jan 22

ACCEDE (ah-seed) approve; concede; yield;
consent and agreement.
Remember: We ACCEPT and CEDE.
Answer: Lionized means to be treated like a famous
person. I know your name because you are famous.

Jan 23

AMOROUS (am-or-us) ardent; attracted; romantic; lusting after another.
Remember: We are in AMOUR or love.
Question: Your dinner is a delicious diminution of a meal. How full are you?

Jan 24

EXPOSTULATE (ex-potch-chew-late) argue; reasoning earnestly with strong protest.
Remember: We EX press and POSTULATE.
Answer: You are not full. Diminution means to get smaller. Your meal is smaller.

Jan 25

MONEY YOU MAY GET,
WHEN YOU ABET

ABET (ah-bet) assist; prod; support;
helping to carry out of a plan.
Remember: We BET you will help.
Question: A denizen comes into the house. You run
out. The denizen chases you down the street. What
are you?

Jan 26

WHEN ANTS
ARE THE
TOPIC,
THEY'RE TOO
SMALL TO
SEE,
THEY'RE SO
MICROSCOPIC,
THEY CAN SNEAK BY ME.

MICROSCOPIC (mike-cro-scop-ick) minute; teeny;
too small to see by the eye.
Remember: MICROSCOPE is needed.
Answer: A robber. A denizen is a resident. The
person lives there and you do not.

Jan 27

The aesthetic flowers made the dog happy.

AESTHETIC (ah-stet-tik) attractive; artistic.
the appreciation of beauty.
Remember: ARTISTIC
Question: I am incurious about the package. I prod and poke it. It has a maroon ribbon. How fast do I open it?

Jan 28

I LIKE TO BRAY,
BECAUSE I'M BOLD,
I DON'T RUN AWAY,
TRUTH BE TOLD.

BRAZEN (bray-zen) audacious; brash; bold;
bold without caring about shame.
Remember: BRAY when bold.
Answer: Not fast at all. Incurious means not being interested.

Jan 29

He lived an ascetic life since he was stranded on a desert island.

ASCETIC (ah-set-tik) austere; stark; frugal;
great self-control
Remember: SCEPTIC will not do it.
Question: You espy a snake. It has speckles and coral eyes. Why don't you run away?

Jan 30

Forbear junk food and you will get in great shape.

FORBEAR (for-bare) avoid; abstain; refrain;
not doing something on purpose.
Remember: FOR it is BARE when we do not do it.
Answer: Espy means to see from far away. It is not near you.

Jan 31

ESCHEW (es-shoo) avoid; shun; abandon; abstaining by staying away.
Remember: ESCAPE CHEW and not eat.
Question: Your friend is lonely. You send her a massive missive. Why does she enjoy it?

Feb 1

SCUTTLEBUTT (skud-del-but) hearsay; rumour; spreading gossip without verifying the truth.
Remember: SCUTTLE by and say BUT.
Answer: You sent her a big letter. A missive is a communication sent by mail.

Feb 2

> ## The coin trick flummoxed me.

FLUMMOX (flum-mux) baffle; puzzle; mystify; confusion or bewilderment.
Remember: FLUB like a dumb OX.
Question: You go to a laudation and bring clothes. Why did your clothes not get cleaned?

Feb 3

> A LAMINA IS A THIN COAT, LIKE PAINT UPON A WALL. OR LILY PADS IN A MOAT, IT COVERS ONE AND ALL.

LAMINA (lam-in-ah) bark; sheet; coat; a coating with a thin layer.
Remember: A LAMB IN A white wool.
Answer: A laudation is a tribute. Someone is praised with a speech at a laudation. No laundry will be washed.

Feb 4

THE RAIN AND WIND ASSAILS THE WINDOWS.

ASSAIL (ah-sale) bash; blast; slam; attacking violently.

Remember: ASSAULT when you attack.

Question: Your friend says his hat is expensive. You say, "Your hat is ignoble." Why does your friend look at you funny?

Feb 5

The diffident child would not come out.

DIFFIDENT (dif-fi-dent) bashful; meek; unsure; lacking in confidence.

Remember: Being DIFFERENT DENTS confidence.

Answer: Ignoble means inferior.

Feb 6

We sat in the natatorium and enjoyed the water.

NATATORIUM (nah-tah-tore-ee-um) bath; pool; swimming pool or bath.
Remember: NATURAL AQUARIUM.
Question: Your car is stagnant. You push the pedal down. It quickly goes at a vapid pace. What do you probably do next?

Feb 7

We came to an estuary but we did not swim.

ESTUARY (es-chew-air-re) bay; gulf; cove; body of water where a river meets the ocean.
Remember: IT'S TO AIRY water.
Answer: Get out of the car. Vapid means being lifeless or unanimated. The car is not moving.

Feb 8

The sunrise, a chick and a sprout are nascent.

NASCENT (na-sent) beginning; promising; growing; new start of a thing that will continue a long time.
Remember: ASCENT with the first step.
Question: You find broccoli to be flocculent. You eat it anyway. A scent wafts from you. Why do I not leave the room?

Feb 9

I don't give credence to monsters. Why do you ask?

CREDENCE (kre-dense) belief; trust; acceptance; believing an idea without evidence
Remember: It's CREDIBLE.
Answer: Flocculent means clumpy like wool. Broccoli is clumpy. The scent is probably perfume.

Feb 10

WHEN YOU CASTIGATE, YOU CAN BE MEAN, MAYBE YOU SHOULD WAIT, AND NOT MAKE A SCENE.

CASTIGATE (cast-ee-gayt) berate; lecture; scold; criticizing in an angry way.

Remember: CAST out and close the GATE.

Question: You have a ram in your bunk. Why do you call it rambunctious?

Feb 11

His acerbic words hurt me.

ACERBIC (ah-sir-bick) bitter; sour; cutting; harsh or acrid attitude.

Remember: ACE at BICKER is a bitter person.

Answer: It is out of control. Rambunctious means loud and out of control.

Feb 12

The man wore an infinitesimal hat that was way too small.

INFINITESIMAL (in-fin-ee-tes-ee-mal) bitty; tiny; tiny or extremely small.

Remember: INFINITELY SMALL.

Question: You say, "This chocolate cake is dank!" Do you eat it?

Feb 13

WHEN YOU REDACT,
WORDS YOU BLACKED OUT,
YOU CHANGED MY ACT,
NOW THE MEANING IS IN DOUBT.

REDACT (re-dakt) black out; obscure; ink out; edit out words by blacking them out.

Remember: RED out FACT.

Answer: No. Dank means: being unpleasantly moist. It is probably too soggy.

Feb 14

Wearing that to a business meeting is a big faux pas.

FAUX PAS (fo-pa) blunder; error; misstep; etiquette mistake, especially in public.
Remember: FAKE PASS we should not make.
Question: I like to cajole you. What am I doing?

Feb 15

The intrepid mouse scared the big cat.

BOO!

INTREPID (in-trep-pid) bold; courageous; valiant; brave and having no fear.
Remember: INTIMIDATE others.
Answer: I am coaxing you. I am using flattery to convince you to do something.

Feb 16

The mouse showed temerity.

TEMERITY (tem-mer-rit-tee) bold; daring; nerve; being foolish and unafraid of danger.
Remember: MERIT praise for ME.
Question: You climb up and addle your horse. You grab the reigns and shout "Tally-ho!" Why don't you go anywhere?

Feb 17

The stalwart cat scared all the dogs.

STALWART (stal-wart) bold; robust; strong; strength and power.
Remember: STALL WART when strong.
Answer: Addle means to confuse. You confused your horse.

Feb 18

VAPID (va-pid) boring; dull; tedious; lifeless or unanimated.
Remember: A VAPOUR IDEA is boring.
Question: The snow is getting ubiquitous. Did it quit snowing?

Feb 19

BANAL (bay-nal) boring; trite; bland; common and dull saying.
Remember: BAN ALL boring sayings.
Answer: No. Ubiquitous means being everywhere. The snow is more everywhere because it is still snowing.

Feb 20

The jaunty boy skipped across the yard.

JAUNTY (jawn-tee) bouncy; brisk; lively;
perky and filled with pleasure.
Remember: JUMPY when happy.
Question: You serve a chicken dinner with verve and
ketchup. Was dinner enjoyable?

Feb 21

I never knew why he was so chary.

CHARY (chairy) cautious; cagey; hesitant;
wary and guarded.
Remember: WARY when cautious.
Answer: Yes. Verve means enthusiasm. You served
it with excitement and energy.

Feb 22

He abraded his hair and noticed a lot of looks.

ABRADE (ah-brayde) chafe; erode; wear; wearing down by rubbing.
Remember: BRAID it by doing it over and over.
Question: You want to adopt a dog. You decide to take a furlough. What kind of dog did you adopt?

Feb 23

The boy like to vacillate between choosing vanilla or chocolate.

VACILLATE (va-sel-layte) change; teeter; seesaw; going back and forth between two extremes.
Remember: VACATE and come back LATER.
Answer: You did not adopt a dog. You took a vacation. A furlough is a vacation or time away from work.

The woman had the strange idiosyncrasy of constantly playing with her earlobes.

IDIOSYNCRASY (id-ee-oh-sink-kras-ee) quirk; physical or mental habit.
Remember: An IDIOT SYNCHRONIZES habits.
Question: I tell you, "You are transparent and nigh to me." How do you know we will talk again?

His jabber made me want to leave.

JABBER (ja-bur) chatter; utter; babble; speaking fast in an unclear way.
Remember: You JAB your words like a BUR.
Answer: Being nigh is to be near. You are close and we will talk again.

Feb 26

The garrulous woman bored us to tears.

GARRULOUS (gar-rule-lus) chatty; blabby; talking about boring or trivial things.
Remember: GARISH when trifles RULE US.
Question: The bride and groom are standing under a gazette on the lawn. It starts raining. Why do they get soaked?

Feb 27

You're voluble like a bull when you are loud.

VOLUBLE (vol-you-bul) chatty; gabby; mouthy; talkative and loud.
Remember: VOLUME is like a BULL.
Answer: A gazette is a newspaper. It hardly covers both of them.

Feb 28

He never minded the loquacious lady.

LOQUACIOUS (lo-qway-she-yowse) chatty; wordy; talking too much or too freely.

Remember: LONG words like AQUA to US.

Question: You vacillate in front of me. Why is it annoying?

Mar 1

The credulous boy believed the cat was really talking.

CREDULOUS (kred-you-lus) gullible; trusting; easily tricked or fooled.

Remember: So CREDIBLE it fools US.

Answer: You change your mind a lot. Vacillate means to go back and forth.

A CALICO TOOK A SEAT,
IN FRONT OF A PICASSO,
I COULD ONLY SEE ITS FEET,
THEY WERE WHITE AS SNOW.

CALICO (kal-lik-ko) checkered; patterned; colorful; different colours and random shapes.
Remember: CALICO cat has many colours.
Question: You worry about the minutia by the hour. How many minutes will you worry?

Mar 3

His pied scarf had many colors and shapes.

PIED (pyed) checkered; speckled; flecked; composed of many colours.
Remember: PIE can be in colorful pieces.
Answer: Not many. Minutia means small details or unimportant things. Small things are nothing to worry about

Mar 4

Jocularity filled the room when he took out the hand puppet.

JOCULARITY (jok-you-lar-rit-tee) cheer; glee; joking in a humorous way.

Remember: JOKE with CLARITY.

Question: You tie a cummerbund in your hair. Why does everyone look at you funny?

Mar 5

THIS IS MY PROGENY,
THE CUTEST LITTLE TYKE.
BECAUSE HE CAME FROM ME,
WE DO LOOK ALIKE,

PROGENY (prodge-gen-nee) children; seed; spawn; descendants or offspring.

Remember: PROGRESS is ANY baby.

Answer: A cummerbund is a sash worn around the waist.

Mar 6

I AM QUITE ROTUND,
AND MY BALL IS ROUND,
I HAVE A LOT OF FUN,
THROWING IT AROUND.

ROTUND (row-tond) chubby; plump; circular; roundly shaped as a perfect sphere.
Remember: ROUND.
Question: You buy geraniums for a decennium. How do I know you bought a lot of geraniums?

Mar 7

The decorous boy won a lot of medals due to his good behavior and good deeds.

DECOROUS (dek-or-us) civilized; conforming; good mannered and well behaved.
Remember: Good DECOR is around US.
Answer: A decennium is a decade. You bought geraniums for a decade. You have lots by now.

GABBLE (ga-bul) clatter; drivel; blab;
unclear noises or incoherent sounds.
Remember: Cannot understand GOBBLE noises.
Question: I flummox you with a stick over and over.
What have I done to you?

ABLUTION (ah-blew-shun) cleansing; washing;
bathing your body with water.
Remember: A SOLUTION cleans us.
Answer: I confused you. Flummox means to confuse
or bewilder. I confused you with a stick over and
over.

Perspicacious boys are not surprised.

PERSPICACIOUS (per-spee-kay-shish) clever;
insightful and wise.
Remember: PERSPECTIVE is TENACIOUS.
Question: There is a white lamina sitting on your car.
You have a leash and a small shovel. How do you get
it off your car?

His platitudes bored us to sleep.

PLATITUDE (pla-tit-tood) cliche; trite; banal;
overused, dull and boring saying.
Remember: FLAT ATTITUDE is boring.
Answer: You shovel it off. The white lamina is snow.

Mar 12

The denouement ended the story.

DENOUEMENT (de-new-mah) finale; ending; climax or conclusion of a complicated drama.
Remember: END comes after MOVEMENT.
Question: You eat dinner with your friend. She burps and says her gestation is done. What will you probably do next?

Mar 13

The boy reached the apex and he was the tallest thing around.

APEX (ay-peks) climax; topmost; highest; uppermost point.
Remember: A PEAK is the highest point.
Answer: Get her to a hospital! She is having a baby! Gestation means being pregnant.

Mar 14

MALADROIT (mal-ah-droyt) clumsy; inept; poorly skilled.
Remember: A MAL ADROIT is poor skill.
Question: You stand by your air conditioner and venerate your living room. Why are you still hot?

Mar 15

INELEGANCE (in-el-leg-ants) coarse; unpolished; crudely ungraceful characteristics.
Remember: It is UN ELEGANT.
Answer: Venerate means to admire. You are admiring your living room. You are not cooling it.

Mar 16

CAJOLE (ka-joel) coax; persuade; entice; persuading by using false flattery.
Remember: A CAGEY OLE friend can persuade.
Question: You sit next to me. You burp and you are eupeptic. Will I be happy sitting next to you?

Mar 17

NEOLOGISM (nee-ol-la-jiz-am) coinage; slang; new phrase or expression.
Remember: A NEW LOG explains an ISM.
Answer: Yes. Eupeptic means to be in good spirits. Happy.

CONFRERE (con-frair) colleague; co-worker; sharing an association with a fellow worker.
Remember: CONTACT with a FRIEND.
Question: You wince because I evince you. You pinch yourself. What have I done to you?

RIPOSTE (re-post) comeback; quip; retort; replying in a fast and sharp way.
Remember: I RIP your POST to shreds.
Answer: I proved something to you. Evince means to prove or show to be true.

Mar 20

There was a strong camaraderie between the two friends.

CAMARADERIE (kam-mar-rod-er-ree) fellowship; close friendships among a group.
Remember: COMRADES with ME.
Question: Would you invite a priggish person to your party? Would they be fun or a drag?

Mar 21

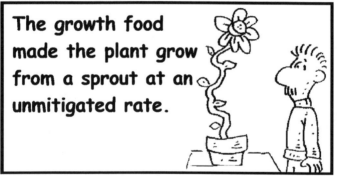

The growth food made the plant grow from a sprout at an unmitigated rate.

UNMITIGATED (un-mit-tee-gayt-ted) complete; total and not reducing.
Remember: UN METERED or GATED.
Answer: No. They would irritate you because they follow all rules and insist you do too.

Mar 22

He showed aplomb because of his umbrella.

APLOMB (ah-plum) confidence; poise; assurance; calmly assured in manner and action.
Remember: A PLUMB job when confident.
Question: You purse your lips and let out an afflatus. You smile at me. Do I leave the room?

Mar 23

He had a sanguine attitude we knew he would get the job done well.

SANGUINE (san-gwin) confident; hopeful; upbeat; optimistic and hopeful.
Remember: SANS WHINE when we hope.
Answer: No. You exhaled a breath. An afflatus is a breath of inspiration.

Mar 24

ABSTRUSE (ab-stroose) confusing; obscure;
profound and difficult to understand.
Remember: ABSOLUTE RUSE.
Question: You find your friend is propertied. Do you
untie your friend?

Mar 25

CABAL (ka-ball) conspirators; club; clique;
secret and mysterious association.
Remember: A CAB ALL to where we meet.
Answer: No. Propertied means rich.

Mar 26

I had to sell my ski stuff because of the invariable sun.

INVARIABLE (in-var-ree-ah-bul) constant; static; inflexible and not changeable.

Remember: UN VARIABLE people stay the same.

Question: You put a hat on your dog. I say: I see your dog is waggish. Your dog is not wagging its tail. Why do we laugh?

Mar 27

The South Pole is antipode to the North Pole.

ANTIPODE (ant-tee-poad) contrary; negative; exact opposites.

Remember: ANTI ODE is an opposite story.

Answer: Waggish means to amuse or make something funny. Your dog is doing something funny.

CONDUCE (kon-doose) contribute; promote; lead; leading to a result.
Remember: A CONDUIT leads to somewhere.
Question: You surfeit all the time. The water is tepid. Why does your surf outfit not fit?

CERTITUDE (sir-ti-tood) surety; assurance; positive with a conviction.
Remember: A CERTAIN ATTITUDE is positive.
Answer: Surfeit means to eat or drink to excess. You became fat and your bathing suit does not fit.

Mar 30

He is a good colleague and we work together for many years now.

COLLEAGUE (col-leag) co-worker; partner; colleague or a fellow worker.
Remember: COLLEGE where we work together.
Question: You abscond a rabbit in a hat. What are you likely to be?

Mar 31

He learned a lesson about being querulous.

QUERULOUS (qwer-rul-lus) crabby; cranky; whining and complaining, a lot and often.
Remember: You QUARREL with US.
Answer: A magician. Abscond means to hide. You hide the rabbit in the hat.

Apr 1

WHEN YOU LUCUBRATE, YOU WILL KNOW THE TOPIC GREAT.

LUCUBRATE (luke-you-brayte) cram; learn; work; studying late at night.
Remember: LOOK and RATE what we study.
Question: You are in a Chinook. There is a drizzle. You are not in a helicopter. What are you flying in?

Apr 2

THE HOUSE IS A POKEY, WHEN THE ROOF DOES POKE ME.

POKEY (po-kee) cramped; confined; shabby; small cramped place.
Remember: So small you can POKE ME.
Answer: A storm. A Chinook is a strong wind or gale.

Apr 3

MOROSE (mor-rowse) cranky; sad; gloomy;
sullenly unhappy and lacking cheer.
Remember: MORE ROSES are needed.
Question: You live on the telluric. How do I know
that I live there too?

Apr 4

IMPUTE (im-pewt) credit; ascribe; assign;
incorrectly blaming someone.
Remember: INCORRECTLY COMPUTE.
Answer: Telluric means "On the earth."

Apr 5

ZENITH (zee-nif) crest; climax; apex;
peaking at the highest point.
Remember: ZEN is a higher state.
Question: Your estate is in a legal estuary. How
much longer will you live there?

Apr 6

ATTENUATE (ah-ten-you-ayte) cripple; reduce;
weakening and getting smaller.
Remember: ATTENTION you ATE becomes small.
Answer: For as long as you own a boat. An estuary is
a narrow body of water.

Apr 7

NEOTERIC (ne-oh-ter-rik) crisp; recent; new; recent in origin and newly existing.

Remember: NEW and TERRIFIC.

Question: The wind is propitious. How fast does your sailboat go?

Apr 8

PIVOTAL (piv-vit-tul) critical; important; crucial; decisive moment affecting your life.

Remember: PIVOT at a VITAL time.

Answer: Not fast. It is gentle. Propitious means being favourable or gentle. Kind.

He had a
nasty barb for
us and it was
very insulting.

BARB (barb) criticism; jibe; insult;
saying insulting and scornful words.
Remember: BARD is sharp and pointed.
Question: Your emails are protean. Are you an email
pro?

His mordant
words will
make you
feel very
small.

MORDANT (mor-dent) cruel; biting; scathing;
replying with mean sarcastic words.
Remember: MORTIFY like an ANT.
Answer: Not really. Your emails change a lot.
Protean means changing in shape or character. Your
emails change. That's all.

Apr 11

There was something a bit recondite about the picture.

RECONDITE (re-kon-dyte) cryptic; secret; mysterious and not easily understood.
Remember: RECON at NIGHT to see the secret.
Question: Your monster needs attention. You remonstrate your monster. Why do you run away?

Apr 12

I know it has side effects but it really is a great elixir.

ELIXIR (ee-liks-er) cure; potion; remedy; exciting invigorating drink.
Remember: Invigorating drink LICKS fatigue.
Answer: You argued with it. Remonstrate means to argue. Never argue with a monster.

Apr 13

PITHY (pith-thee) curt; concise; terse;
forceful aggressive attitude.
Remember: PIT against THEE.
Question: You are my confrere. Do you always agree
with me?

Apr 14

DANK (dank) damp; humid; muggy;
musty and soaking wet.
Remember: DUNK and get wet.
Answer: Maybe. A confrere is a fellow worker.
Maybe you agree and maybe you do not.

Apr 15

METE (meet) deal; disperse; dole;
giving something by dividing it.
Remember: MEET to give something.
Question: I wake up. I raise my hands and say, "I am enervated!" What will I probably do next?

Apr 16

PERFIDIOUS (per-fid-ee-us) deceitful; disloyal;
acting untrustworthy and unfaithful.
Remember: INSIDIOUS people betray US.
Answer: Go back to bed! Enervated means to be tired or worn out. You need more sleep.

Apr 17

His duplicity was obvious because the money vanished only when he was around.

DUPLICITY (dew-plis-sit-tee) deceit; sneaky; telling lies or double speaking.
Remember: DUPLICATE tricks us, have PITY.
Question: I have an animus. You have an animus. Does everyone have an animus?

Apr 18

A canon in our house is to pick up wet towels.

CANON (can-non) decree; law; rule; collection of rules.
Remember: What you CAN do when rules are ON.
Answer: No. Animus means having hatred. A lot of people don't have one. The sun is shinning. It's a sunny day!

Apr 19

ASPERSION (ah-spur-shun) defame; libel; slander; telling a lie to hurt a reputation.
Remember: ASP PERSON tells lies.
Question: You have a progeny. When is it a prodigy?

Apr 20

APOSTATE (ah-pa-stayte) defector; revolt; heretic; abandoning a connection to a party or faith.
Remember: Membership in a POST STATE.
Answer: When your child is a genius. Progeny means offspring. Prodigy means genius.

DESICCATE (des-ee-kayt) dehydrate; scorch; preserving by drying up water.
Remember: DESERT ATE the water.
Question: You wear an ostentatious hat. Why might you look like an ostrich?

MIEN (meen) demeanour; bearing; countenance; attitude or manner.
Remember: Nice and MEAN are manners.
Answer: Your hat is flashy. It may have ostrich feathers because ostrich feathers are flashy.

Apr 23

The obtuse robot was bad at math.

OBTUSE (ob-toose) dense; dumb; slow;
dull thinking and obtuse.
Remember: OBJECT to a USE we don't understand.
Question: You amalgamate a white sock and a black
sock. What animal do you look like?

Apr 24

I gainsay your cookie theft accusation.

GAINSAY (gayne-say) deny; controvert; refute;
contradicting or challenging.
Remember: GAIN when we SAY no.
Answer: A zebra. Amalgamate means to blend or
combine. You are wearing black and white like the
colours of a zebra.

Apr 25

DECLIVITY (dee-kliv-at-tee) descent; dip;
downhill and declining slope.
Remember: DECLINE and become BITTY.
Question: You draw a smiley face. Is it facile?

Apr 26

ABHOR (ab-bor) despise; loathe; detest;
intensely hating.
Remember: ABSOLUTE HORROR we dislike.
Answer: Facile means easy to do. Drawing smiley
faces is easy.

INDIGENT (in-dee-gent) destitute; impoverished; broke and living with little money.
Remember: A hobo is an INDEPENDENT GENT.
Question: You read a histrionic book. What kind of book is it?

DIGRESS (di-gres) deviate; meander; roam; changing a new topic.
Remember: PROGRESS to a new topic.
Answer: It is a dramatic book. It means dramatic or spectacular.

Apr 29

FEALTY (feel-tee) devoted; dedicated; allegiance; loyal and faithful.

Remember: FEEL like TEA with a friend.

Question: We walk to the natatorium and I ask, "Do you like plants?" What kind of exercise will we probably get?

Apr 30

ANTONYM (an-ton-nim) reverse; negative; contrary and opposite.

Remember: ANTI NAME is the opposite.

Answer: Swimming. A natatorium is an indoor pool.

May 1

It was a grand regale and we had fun.

REGALE (re-gayle) dinner; banquet; entertain; grand entertaining party.
Remember: REGAL festival is a party.
Question: I give you a thousand dollars. You aggrandize it and give it back to me. Am I happy?

May 2

He showed tact by bringing a cracker.

TACT (takt) diplomacy; skill; perception; carefully and thoughtfully acting.
Remember: ACT at the right time.
Answer: Yes. You give me more. Aggrandize means to make bigger.

May 3

My report may inveigh you a bit.

INVEIGH (in-vay) discredit; shame; dishonour; attacking with harsh criticism.

Remember: INVADE when we criticize.

Question: I approach from the left. You reproach from the right. Why may we never meet?

May 4

Your eyes belie where the ball may hide.

BELIE (be-lye) disguise; misrepresent; disprove; proving a lie to be false.

Remember: BE a LIE and we know the truth.

Answer: Reproach means to blame or find fault. We may never meet. You are just blaming me.

May 5

PEJORATIVE (pa-jaw-ra-tiv) disparage; demean; derogatory insulting words.
Remember: PEEVE and ORATE anger.
Question: You drink a soda with sodality. Why does the soda taste better?

May 6

SOLICITUDE (so-lis-sit-tood) disquiet; uneasiness; worried and anxious.
Remember: SOLO ATTITUDE makes worry.
Answer: You are drinking it with friends. Sodality means comrades.

May 7

I have an eclectic collection of pets.

ECLECTIC (ee-klek-tik) diverse; broad; varied; many styles or types.
Remember: Say EEK when HECTIC.
Question: I said something smart. You gainsay me. Did you gain anything from what I said?

May 8

A cetacean stopped by and said hello.

CETACEAN (see-tay-shun) dolphin; whale; blowhole aquatic mammal.
Remember: Dolphin lives in SEA or OCEAN.
Answer: Gainsay means to contradict. You denied what I said and countered it with an argument.

May 9

COMP (komp) donation; perk; freebie; getting a complimentary gift.
Remember: COMPLIMENTARY gift.
Question: You see your faux face in a faucet. What happened to your face?

May 10

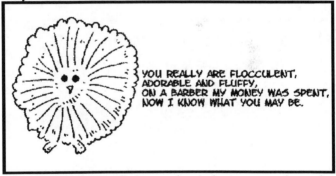

FLOCCULENT (flok-you-lent) downy; wooly; tuft; fluffy and soft.
Remember: FLOCK of fluffy clouds.
Answer: Nothing. You see your reflection. It's fake because it is a reflection. Faux means fake.

May 11

HISTRIONIC (his-tree-on-ick) dramatic; theatrical; melodramatic and insincere.

Remember: HISTORY is BIONIC when fake.

Question: You're at the museum. There is a brontosaurus, a stegosaurus and an ignoramus. Why do you leave?

May 12

BABBLE (ba-bul) drivel; incoherent; inarticulate; foolish chattering and talking.

Remember: BABY says BULL and nothing.

Answer: An ignoramus is a dumb person who thinks they are smart. They say dumb things in a pushy way.

May 13

A PHLEGMATIC PERSON IS NOT ANNOYED BY A PESKY BIRD. EXPECT NO REACTION.

PHLEGMATIC (fleg-mat-tik) dull; sluggish; unconcerned and not excited to action.
Remember: FLEDGE AUTOMATICALLY boring.
Question: You fructify a tomato plant. You put it in a glass and stir. Why can't you drink it?

May 14

The cactus was the only thing in the hot arid desert.

ARID (ah-rid) dusty; barren; parched; dry such as a desert.
Remember: RID of water.
Answer: Fructify means to bear fruit. You fertilized it. You will get baby tomatoes. Not juice.

May 15

He whistled with alacrity and walked with a bounce in his step.

ALACRITY (ah-lak-rit-tee) eagerness; alertness; readily cheerful and eager.
Remember: Happy when our LACKS are ITTY.
Question: You drink imitation lemonade. You make a limitation for orange juice. Which will you drink more of?

May 16

I ameliorated my computer problem by plugging it in.

AMELIORATE (ah-meal-ee-or-rate) ease; mend; relieving and making it better.
Remember: A MEAL RATES better.
Answer: The lemonade. Limitation means to set a limit. You set a limit on how much orange juice you will drink.

May 17

Drawing smiley faces is facile.

FACILE (fa-sil) effortless; hasty; simplistic;
easy to master.
Remember: FACES are SILLY simple.
Question: When does incense, incense you?

May 18

Maybe exit would have been a bit better.

EGRESS

EGRESS (ee-gres) emerge; departure; escape;
exit to the street.
Remember: PROGRESS out the exit.
Answer: When you don't like the smell. Incense
means to make angry. Incense also is burned to make
a pleasant odour.

May 19

TERMINUS (term-min-nus) end; limit; boundary; end of a train line or bus route.
Remember: TERMINATE for US at the end.
Question: You sit on something commodious. What are you sitting on?

May 20

ABSCOND (ab-skond) escape; flee; run away; leaving quickly to avoid arrest.
Remember: SCOUNDREL runs away.
Answer: You are sitting on something large with a lot of space. Commodious means being roomy and spacious.

May 21

He jumped on a lark and had a lot of fun.

LARK (lahr-k) escape; risky; spree;
going on a whim without thinking first.
Remember: Road is DARK but we go.
Question: Do you feel splenetic because the day is splendid?

May 22

Evanescent smoke is much better.

EVANESCENT (ev-van-nes-sent) evaporating;
fading and vanishing like vapour.
Remember: VANISH like a SCENT.
Answer: No. You feel less splenetic. Splenetic means gloomy or sullen. A splendid day makes you happy.

The cake was ambrosial because it was creamy and moist.

AMBROSIAL (am-bro-she-al) excellent; luscious; divine and pleasing to taste.
Remember: AMBROSIA is delicious.
Question: I tell you a fable. You say, "You are affable." Am I laughable or do you like me?

The wind became immoderate.

IMMODERATE (im-mod-er-rate) excessive; extravagant and unrestrained in size or enormity.
Remember: UN MODERATE is big.
Answer: You like me. Affable means being polite and friendly. An affable person is likeable.

May 25

We will canvas the town and find your cat.

CANVASS (kan-vas) explore; seek; sift; searching well and thoroughly.

Remember: CAN look VAST to find it.

Question: You write and your compunction is strong. I say, "You have punctuation errors!" Why did I say that?

May 26

The prodigal son spent a lot of money.

PRODIGAL (prod-de-gal) extravagant; lavish; excessively reckless with money.

Remember: buy PRODUCTS by the GALLON.

Answer: You probably have errors. Compunction means a feeling of regret for your actions. It has nothing to do with punctuation.

May 27

CONFABULATION (con-fab-you-lay-shun)
fabrication; chitchat; gossip;
telling a made-up story.
Remember: CON and FABRICATE a story.
Question: Your dog's hair is long. You upbraid your
dog. Why is your dog mad at you?

May 28

FAUX (fo) false; mock; sham;
fake and not real.
Remember: FAKE.
Answer: Upbraid means to scold or blame. You're
dog is sulking. Be nice to your doggy!

May 29

He wore his swank new clothes to the party.

SWANK (swanc) fancy; Swagger; Grand; elegant and showy.

Remember: SWAN is pretty.

Question: You brook, a brook. Did you enjoy your swim?

May 30

WHEN YOU SAY ENERVATE,
I KNOW YOU ARE TIRED,
TOO MUCH ON YOUR PLATE,
YOUR ENERGY EXPIRED.

ENERVATE (en-er-vayte) fatigue; weaken; exhaust; wearing out and making tired.

Remember: Our ENERGY EVAPORATES.

Answer: No. Brook means to endure. Brook also means a small river. You endured a small stream. It may be too cold.

May 31

The repast was refreshing.

REPAST (re-past) feast; meal; drink;
food or anything restorative.
Remember: RE do the PAST when we feel good.
Question: Does a person give to charity when they
are chary?

Jun 1

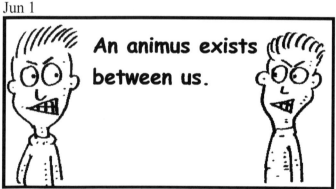

An animus exists between us.

ANIMUS (an-ne-mus) feud; dislike; animosity;
hating something or someone.
Remember: ANIMOSITY between US.
Answer: No. Chary means frugal. It also means to be
cautious and not reckless. They do not give away
money.

Jun 2

The mercurial man changed his mind.

MERCURIAL (mer-cure-re-al) fickle; volatile; moody and unpredictable.
Remember: A thermometer MERCURY changes.
Question: You write a poem that is two pages long. You ask me to add an erratum. Why do I refuse?

Jun 3

Bringing a parrot was apposite.

APPOSITE (app-o-sit) fitting; relevant; suited; applicable or apt.
Remember: APPROPRIATE.
Answer: An erratum is an error or a mistake in writing. Why would I add that?

Jun 4

He soon realized the tattoo was irrevocable.

IRREVOCABLE (ear-re-voke-ah-bul)
fixed; immutable; irreversible;
not changeable and irrevocable.
Remember: ERROR when you REVOKE.
Question: You blandish me. Do I feel bland?

Jun 5

He blandished his dad for the car keys.

BLANDISH (blan-dish) flatter; entice; kind;
persuading good flattery.
Remember: OUTLANDISH.
Answer: No. Blandish means to make someone feel
better by saying good words. I feel grand.

Jun 6

The transient cat was gone the next day.

TRANSIENT (tran-see-ent) fleeting; flash; brief; existing for a short time and disappearing.
Remember: TRANSMIT SENT.
Question: A duck quacks loudly. You shout and run toward towards an egress and a tern. Why do I call you a coward?

Jun 7

I never knew why my balloon flights were always ephemeral.

EPHEMERAL (ee-fem-er-ral) fleeting; momentary; existing for a short time.
Remember: Flicker like an EMERALD.
Answer: Egress is an exit. You got scared by a quacking duck and ran away.

Jun 8

The tractable dog was very obedient.

TRACTABLE (tract-ah-bul) flexible; compliant; meekly obedient and manageable.
Remember: On TRACK we are ABLE.
Question: You're in a boat. A strong assail is apparent. There is a reef ahead. Why don't you see it?

Jun 9

It was serendipity when money arrived in the mail because I was not expecting it.

SERENDIPITY (ser-rend-dip-pit-tee) fluke; lucky; unexpected fortunate find.
Remember: SURE to END your PITY.
Answer: Assail means to attack violently. You're too busy fighting to look for reefs.

Jun 10

The robot was an ignoramus when it came to the rules of chess.

IGNORAMUS (ig-nor-ram-mus) fool; stupid; dunce; dumb without knowing it.
Remember: IGNORANT and AMUSED.
Question: I bake bread. I say, "You probably don't want some. You look aloof." Do you eat my bread?

Jun 11

A QUIXOTIC PERSON ACTS LIKE A FOOL AND IS UNPREDICTABLE.

QUIXOTIC (qwiks-ot-tic) foolish; unrealistic; impulsively impractical and unpredictable.
Remember: QUICK to be NEUROTIC.
Answer: You say, "I like bread. I am not indifferent to it." Then you eat some. Being aloof means you are not uninterested.

Jun 12

The brouhaha was a lof of fun and everyone had a good time.

BROUHAHA (brew-ha-ha) fracas; uproar; brawl; ruckus or commotion.
Remember: Drink BREW and say, "HA-HA".
Question: You take your dog to a vet and you castigate him. You give him a treat. Why does he forgive you?

Jun 13

IT'S LIKE A COMEDY, WHEN WITH A FRIEND, WE HAVE GREAT COMITY, FROM BEGINNING TO END.

COMITY (com-mit-tee) friendly; coexisting; peaceful and harmonious relationship.
Remember: COMEDY when friendly.
Answer: Castigate means to chastise using a punishment. You only scolded him. You gave him a treat and he forgave you.

AFFABLE (af-ah-bul) friendly; pleasant; easygoing; likable and approachable.

Remember: Tell A FABLE to a friend.

Question: You won the lottery. You say you want to share it. Your words are euphonious. Are you honest?

AMICABLE (amik-ah-bul) friendly; polite; harmonious agreeable solution.

Remember: On a MIKE over a CABLE we agree.

Answer: You are honest. Euphonious means saying pleasant sounding words. I liked your words.

Jun 16

He felt trepidation when he realized he was wearing his new clothes.

TREPIDATION (trep-pid-day-shun) fright; trembling fear and apprehension.
Remember: TREMBLE from INTIMIDATION.
Question: A pachyderm knocked into my tachometer. How did you guess it is a hippo?

Jun 17

Levity filled the room with laughter.

LEVITY (lev-it-tee) giddy; mirth; amusement. enjoying happy things.
Remember: LEVITATE our spirits.
Answer: A tachometer measures water flow. Hippos live in the water.

Jun 18

GLIMPSE (glimps) glance; look; spy;
looking at something briefly.
Remember: GLIMMER is brief.
Question: A genius and a dolt with an idiosyncrasy
are standing outside. How many are standing there?

Jun 19

PHOSPHORESCENCE (fos-for-res-sense) glow;
shinning luminous light.
Remember: PHOSPHOR ESSENCE glows.
Answer: Two. An Idiosyncrasy is a physical or
mental habit. An Idiosyncrasy is not a person. It is a
characteristic.

He always lionized
his son to anyone
who listened.

LIONIZE (lie-on-nized) glorify; celebrate; idolize;
treating a person as if they are famous.
Remember: LION in our EYES.
Question: You wake up at night. You realize the
zeitgeist is wearing all white. Why are you not scared
of it?

She had a
surfeit of
birds and she
always
had
one.

SURFEIT (sir-fit) glut; satiety; excess;
excessive amount.
Remember: Do it again like the SURF and FIT it all.
Answer: A Zeitgeist is the spirit of the time or the
style of a generation. Wearing white is a style.

Jun 22

YOU ARE BENIGNANT,
AND TREAT THEM WELL,
YOU NEVER RANT,
AND YOU NEVER YELL.

BENIGNANT (be-nig-nant) gracious; good; kindly; kind and gracious leader.
Remember: BENEFICIAL GIANT is a good leader.
Question: You react badly when I redact your second act. Why did you react badly?

Jun 23

It was an easy supposition that he broke the window.

SUPPOSITION (sup-oh-sish-shun) guesswork; believing a speculation without evidence.
Remember: SUPPOSE your POSITION.
Answer: I blacked out lines in the second act of your play. Redact means to edit out. I ruined it.

Jun 24

The look of compunction told me who took the money.

COMPUNCTION (com-punk-shun) guilt; remorseful guilt and repentance.
Remember: COMPLAINING PUNK feels guilty.
Question: You go for a drive. You have to devoid a truck. You are exasperated. How do I know the truck is empty?

Jun 25

The elephant would also quaff my coffee in the morning.

QUAFF (kwaf) gulp; swig; guzzle; gulping a beverage quickly.
Remember: LAUGH when we drink.
Answer: Devoid means making vacant or being empty. You emptied the truck.

Jun 26

WE GO DOWN A DELL,
AND IT'S VERY WIDE,
IT'S DEEP LIKE A WELL,
UNTIL THE OTHER SIDE

DELL (del) hallow; dale; ravine;
small valley covered with grass or trees.
Remember: DECLINE into a valley.
Question: You find a treasure map. You say, "This is
not esoteric." Do you find the treasure?

Jun 27

Your sedulous work
has paid off.

A+

SEDULOUS (said-you-lus) hard-working; busy;
actively paying persistent attention.
Remember: SAID you LUST to know.
Answer: Yes. Esoteric means only understood by
those who have the secret. It's not esoteric because
you can understand the map.

Jun 28

SPARTAN (spar-tan) hardy; brave; simple;
able to do without fancy things.
Remember: Eat SPARSE and become TAN.
Question: You stand at a newsstand, notwithstanding
your brother. Are you in good standing with your
brother?

Jun 29

BELLIGERENT (be-lidge-er-rent) hostile;
contentiously combative and prone to war.
Remember: Ring the BELL of a GENT.
Answer: No. Notwithstanding means "in spite of."
You stand there despite your brother standing there
too.

Jun 30

GARGANTUAN (gar-gan-chew-wan) huge; giant; massive and large.

Remember: GARAGE for big things.

Question: A sailor shows you where his navel is. He is standing on a submarine. How do you know he is not wearing a shirt?

Jul 1

HUMONGOUS (you-mong-us) huge; tremendous; immense and big.

Remember: HUGE and MONGO.

Answer: A navel is a belly button. He is not wearing a shirt because you can see it.

Jul 2

KINDLE (kin-dul) ignite; inflame; encourage; sparking interest and excitement.
Remember: KINDLING sticks start fires.
Question: Your friend bets you will help him. You think about it and you abet him. Did he win the bet?

Jul 3

INCULCATE (in-cul-kayte) impart; educate; instil; teaching persistently and earnestly.
Remember: Take IN and CALCULATE teaching.
Answer: Yes. Abet means to help someone to do something.

Jul 4

The caprice of the weather is amazing.

CAPRICE (ca-preese) impulsive; unpredictable;
changing and inspired on a whim.
Remember: CAUSE PRICES are unpredictable.
Question: What is a pivotal moment?

Jul 5

THE FLOWERS ARE INEFFABLE,
BECAUSE THEY ARE SO PRETTY,
OF WORDS I AM INCAPABLE,
ISN'T THAT A PITY.

INEFFABLE (in-ef-ah-bul) unspeakable;
indescribable with words.
Remember: INEPT at telling a FABLE.
Answer: A pivotal moment is a crucial moment
where you have to make an important decision.

Jul 6

He was incurious about the package and he never opened it.

INCURIOUS (in-cure-re-owse) indifferent; apathetic lack of interest.
Remember: UN CURIOUS.
Question: You sit in solicitude. People are all around you. How is that possible?

Jul 7

I discovered my paperclip collection was nugatory in value.

NUGATORY (new-ga-tor-re) ineffectual; trifling; valueless and of little importance.
Remember: NUGGET STORY is not important.
Answer: Solicitude means to worry. You are sitting and worrying with people around you.

Jul 8

INAPT (in-apt) inept; clumsy; amiss;
not appropriate or inapt actions.
Remember: Stays IN our APARTMENT when bad.
Question: You always have invariable weather. What
don't you ever watch on television?

Jul 9

IMBUE (imm-byou) instil; ingrain; inspire;
persuading to a good opinion.
Remember: IN love with BEAU who teaches.
Answer: The Weather Channel. Invariable means
always the same.

Jul 10

EDIFICATION (ed-dee-fi-kay-shun) instruction; uplifting moral teachings.
Remember: EDITORIAL gave an EDUCATION.
Question: You go through an egress. What did you go through?

Jul 11

A didactic story keeps me safe.

DIDACTIC (dye-dak-tik) instructive; preachy; enlightening lesson in a story.
Remember: I DID ACT after learning.
Answer: An exit.

Jul 12

ASPERITY (ah-spare-it-tee) irritable; sternness; severely exhibiting a harsh attitude.
Remember: ASPIRIN TEA because I am irritable.
Question: When does time make you timorous?

Jul 13

EUPHORIA (you-for-re-ya) joy; glee; elation; happily enjoying a good feeling.
Remember: YOU say "yay" FOR YAH.
Answer: When you are late. Timorous means being afraid.

Jul 14

ATTUNE (ah-toon) kinship; being in tune; harmonious relationship.
Remember: Sing A TUNE with others.
Question: You visit the hinterland. What don't you get a hint of?

Jul 15

SYCOPHANT (sik-ko-fant) lackey; servile; flunky; flattering with lies for gain.
Remember: SICKO PANTS as he flatters.
Answer: People. Hinterland is the remote part of a country where no one lives.

Jul 16

MUNIFICENCE (mune-nif-ee-sents) lavish; benevolently generous and giving a lot.
Remember: MONEY to you is just CENTS.
Question: You brew up a big brouhaha. What have you made?

Jul 17

FURLOUGH (fur-lo) layoff; leave; vacation; temporary layoff for rest.
Remember: Wear a FUR when we GO.
Answer: You brewed up an uproar. It's a ruckus or a commotion.

Jul 18

TYRO (tie-row) learner; amateur; novice;
beginner or rookie who makes mistakes.
Remember: TYKE ROW is a child level.
Question: Your turtle has a hard shell. It is fully
amorous. Why is it not afraid of the bigger turtle?

Jul 19

ORATOR (or-ray-tor) lecturer; speaker; spellbinder;
person who speaks well.
Remember: ORAL TOUR.
Answer: Amorous means to be romantic or in love.
You don't fight when you're in love.

Jul 20

ABATEMENT (ah-bayt-ment) lessening;
diminishing to the point of ending.
Remember: BASEMENT is where the house ENDS.
Question: You wear a sweater. Are you demure
because it is azure?

Jul 21

DIMINUTION (dim-min-new-shun) lessening;
weakening and declining to a low point.
Remember: DIMINISH to NOTHING.
Answer: No. Azure is a blue colour. Demure means
shy. The colour makes no difference.

HAUGHTY (haw-tee) lordly; imperious; arrogant; condescending proud attitude.

Remember: HEIGHT above ME.

Question: You can't stop sneezing. You go to the doctor to get an anecdote. Does your sneezing stop?

Jul 23

OSTENTATIOUS (os-tent-tay-shis) loud; garish; flamboyantly gaudy and flashy.

Remember: OSTRICH is flashy.

Answer: No. An anecdote is a funny story. It does not cure colds.

Jul 24

REMUNERATIVE (re-mewn-er-ra-tiv) lucrative; gainfully profiting a great amount.

Remember: REPEAT MONEY when ACTIVE.

Question: I glance it. You glimpse it. Who sees more of it?

Jul 25

TEPID (tep-pid) lukewarm; moderate; apathetic; warm and moderate.

Remember: PIDDLE is not much.

Answer: I do. A glance is longer than a glimpse. I saw more of it.

Jul 26

The cats made euphonious music and everyone like it.

EUPHONIOUS (you-fone-ee-us) lyrical; pleasing harmonious words or sounds.
Remember: EUPHORIC sounds come from US.
Question: You find a comp in your camp. Why might you put out the campfire?

Jul 27

Her mammoth hair was impressive.

MAMMOTH (mam-moth) massive; large; big; huge in size.
Remember: MAM and MOTHER are bigger.
Answer: You leave and go use the comp. A comp is a coupon for getting free stuff.

RUMINATE (room-in-ate) meditate; brainstorm; considering by thinking hard.
Remember: Think in a ROOM and be INNATE.
Question: You're an inamorata. Why would a man walk ten miles in the snow?

AMALGAMATE (ah-mal-ga-mayte) meld; alloy; combining together in a mix.
Remember: MALLS MATE and become one.
Answer: He wants to leave flowers on your doorstep. An inamorata is a woman who is loved. That's why.

Jul 30

MISSIVE (mis-siv) memo; note; letter; communication sent by mail.
Remember: MISS you I HAVE, so I sent a letter.
Question: Can you stand oculus to oculus with an octopus?

Jul 31

BLITHE (blythe) merry; jovial; Cheerful; Ignorantly happy.
Remember: At BIRTH we are happy.
Answer: Yes. An oculus is an eye. You are looking eye-to-eye.

> **The fastidious man always arranged his stuff to point in the same direction.**

FASTIDIOUS (fast-tid-ee-owse) meticulous; picky; doing an exacting task with great care and thought.
Remember: FAST is HIDEOUS.
Question: You are contrarian to being a culinarian. What don't you like to do?

> I USE TO LIVE ON THE EARTH NOW I AM AN EXPATRIATE
>
> I DON'T LIVE THERE ANY MORE

EXPATRIATE (ex-pay-tree-at) migrant; refugee; leaving a country and becoming an outcast.
Remember: EX PATRIOT lives in a new country.
Answer: Cook. A culinarian is a chef. Contrarian means a person who is opposed to something. You are opposed to being a cook.

Aug 3

MIMIC (mim-mik) mime; copycat; imitate;
copying the actions of another.
Remember: A MIME impersonates people.
Question: You recite prose and then repose. What are you doing now?

Aug 4

ABJECT (ab-jekt) miserable; wretched; dismal;
ruined in a hopeless low state.
Remember: ABSOLUTE REJECT.
Answer: Sleeping. Repose means to sleep.

Aug 5

He found an erratum and had to fix it.

ERRATUM (err-rat-tum) misprint; typo; error; making a mistake in writing.
Remember: Make an ERROR and need a TUMS.
Question: A Felis Catus sits in your garden. Do you have to water it?

Aug 6

A caliginous cloud obstructed my view.

CALIGINOUS (kah-lidge-en-us) misty; murky; dark and gloomy.
Remember: CALL out like GIN to US.
Answer: No. It's a cat. Why water a cat?

Aug 7

He kept a miniature robot on his desk.

MINIATURE (min-ee-at-chur) model; mini; tiny; extremely small.
Remember: MINI CHARACTER is a replica.
Question: You smile and hand it to me when I wipe my face with it. Why?

Aug 8

His birth was ignoble since both his parents were frogs.

IGNOBLE (ig-no-bel) modest; peasant; unworthy; inferior birth or position.
Remember: ICKY NOBLE is born poor.
Answer: You're happy because you gave it back. Snaffle means to steal. You took it. I got it back. Nice and clean.

Aug 9

MENDICANT (mend-dee-kant) monk; hobo; begging panhandler.
Remember: MEND I CAN'T this poverty.
Question: I read you a didactic story. Did you like it?

Aug 10

PROBITY (pro-bit-tee) morality; sincerity; rightness; trustworthy and honest.
Remember: PROBE for lies and find ITTY.
Answer: Yes. A didactic story is informative and improves your morale.

Aug 11

He would soon have an impetus to start dancing.

IMPETUS (imp-pit-tus) motivation; incentive; catalyst encouraging to action.

Remember: IMPRESS by PETTING US.

Answer: Loquacious means to talk too much and too freely. You're probably boring me.

Aug 12

I own a horse, a dog and etcetera.

ETCETERA (et-set-er-ah) more; additional; etc; referencing unlisted extras.

Remember: Add EXTRA to what we said.

Question: You're loquacious and gracious. Why do I put space between us?

PROTEAN (pro-tee-an) multifaceted; elastic; changing in shape or variety.
Remember: A PRO TEEN is good at changing.
Question: I am incredulous because you are sedulous. What did I say?

BATHOS (ba-those) mushy; sentimental; gooey; funny sudden event in a serious story.
Remember: A BATH with "OHS" is romantic.
Answer: I am amazed because you are paying attention. Sedulous means paying persistent attention.

Aug 15

The boy offered a mea culpa.

MEA CULPA (may-ah-kul-pa) my mistake; admitting a personal error.

Remember: Guilt makes ME CULPABLE.

Question: Do you have an education in edification?

Aug 16

It was a conundrum as to why he never could finish a puzzle.

CONUNDRUM (con-nun-drum) mystery; puzzle; confusing problem or riddle.

Remember: A CON DRUMS me out.

Answer: You do if you are schooled in something uplifting.

The timorous man screamed and jumped up on the chair.

TIMOROUS (tim-or-rus) nervous; apprehensive; scared and fearful.

Remember: TIMID is US.

Question: You play a game against another team. You ameliorate them. Why aren't you happy?

Aug 18

There is a nexus between the two of us.

NEXUS (neks-us) network; union; connection; link or connection between two groups.

Remember: NEXT to US when we are linked.

Answer: Ameliorate means to improve something. You made them better.

NEOPHYTE (ne-oh-fite) newcomer; novice; trainee; person who makes mistakes due to inexperience.

Remember: NEW to the FIGHT.

Question: You close your eyes and hold out your hand. You feel the ennui. Why don't you like it?

MISNOMER (mis-nohm-er) nickname; misname; Incorrectly saying a name or word.

Remember: MISS NAME.

Answer: Ennui means to feel bored. It's not much fun holding out your arms and getting tired.

PETTIFOGGER (pet-tee-fog-er) nitpicker; quibbler; person who argues about trivia.

Remember: PETTY and FOGGY talking is trivial.

Question: I say, "You are apposite to a fun party." Why do you smile?

Aug 22

EPISTLE (ee-pis-el) note; letter; communication; message sent by messenger.

Remember: EPIC MISSILE.

Answer: Apposite means being relevant to or a good match. Where you thinking opposite?

MULTIFARIOUS (mol-tee-fair-ee-us) varied; numerous parts or diversity.

Remember: MANY and VARIOUS things.

Question: In pedagogy, a parable should not be quixotic. What did I say?

CORPULENT (kor-pew-lent) obese; chubby; plump; large, fat and impressive.

Remember: CORE is PLUMP when full.

Answer: In the art of teaching, a story with a moral should not be a puzzle.

Aug 25

ESPY (es-pee) observe; look; perceive;
seeing from far away.
Remember: I SPY when I look from far away.
Question: Is the word "Enigma", an enigma?

Aug 26

OCCLUDE (oh-clewd) obstruct; conceal; block;
hide from view.
Remember: OCULAR and only get a CLUE.
Answer: It is, if you did not know what Enigma
means. An enigma is a riddle.

Snow in the summer was an anomaly that usually did not happen.

ANOMALY (ah-nom-al-ee) odd; deviation; rarity; out of the ordinary.

Remember: ABNORMAL.

Question: You sing a ditty about a rotund object that taught us about gravity. What are you singing about?

It was preternatural to see rabbits in a tree.

PRETERNATURAL (pre-ter-natch-er-ral) odd; otherworldly and beyond natural.

Remember: Strange when PRE NATURAL.

Answer: An apple. Rotund means round. The story goes: A falling apple gave Newton the idea about gravity.

The ubiquitous birds made him afraid.

UBIQUITOUS (you-bik-wah-tis) omnipresent;
existing everywhere at the same time.
Remember: UBBER and it does not QUIT US.
Question: You descry a book on your bookshelf.
Why don't you have any tears?

I LIKE YOUR OCULUS,
YOU'RE A LUCKY GUY,
WHEN YOU BUY A SUNGLASS,
IT'S ONLY FOR ONE EYE.

OCULUS (ock-you-lus) opening; headlight; eyeball;
an eye.
Remember: BINOCULAR.
Answer: Descry means to see something. You just
found a new book.

Aug 31

He was dogmatic in his thinking that tophats would come back into fashion.

DOGMATIC (dog - mat - tik) opinionated; stubborn; unbendingly believing without proof.
Remember: DOG AUTOMATICALLY grabs on.
Question: You probably use a lexicon every day. What is it?

Sep 1

It was a propitious day because I earned a lot of money.

PROPITIOUS (pro-pish-us) opportune; favourable; conveniently advantageous.
Remember: PROFIT when it is an IOU.
Answer: A dictionary. Each time you spell check, you're using a lexicon.

Sep 2

It turned out to be a fortuitous day after all.

FORTUITOUS (for-to-ah-tis) opportune; fortunate; timely, lucky and unexpected.
Remember: FORTUNATE for US.
Question: You have amazing equanimity. What am I amazed by?

Sep 3

They have polarized views.

UP

DOWN

POLARIZED (pole-ar-rised) opposite; inverse; two contrary opposites.
Remember: POLAR is opposite the artic.
Answer: I am amazed by your calm composure. Equanimity means to have patience or composure.

Sep 4

She wore a
bright florid
hats that had
a lot of colors.

FLORID (flor-id) ornate; blooming; rosy;
flowery looking.
Remember: FLOWER ID.
Question: You quaff. I laugh. What was funny?

Sep 5

His t.v. was anachronistic
but it still worked well.

ANACHRONISTIC (anna-cron-nist-tik) dated;
archaic and existing out of place.
Remember: ANTI CHRONICLE in a time period.
Answer: You gulped down a drink. Quaff means to
drink quickly.

Sep 6

I LIVE IN THE HINTERLAND,
IT'S A LONELY HABIT,
SO I'LL START A BAND,
WITH A MOUSE AND A RABBIT.

HINTERLAND (hint-ur-land) outback; sticks; bush; country backwoods with no one around.

Remember: A HINT of people lives in this LAND.

Question: What kind of bulge does effulge in a dark room?

Sep 7

The piranha was a pariah and he had no friends.

PARIAH (pah-rye-ya) outcast; outsider; exile; unlikable lonely person.

Remember: A PIRANHA has no friends.

Answer: A light bulb does effulge in a dark room. Effulge means to shine with an abundance of light.

Sep 8

The aforementioned instructions told us what to do first.

AFOREMENTIONED (ah-for-ment-shuned) past; previously mentioned.
Remember: BEFORE we MENTIONED it.
Question: I perform an ablation on a pile of leaves. What have I done?

Sep 9

The showed equanimity to the dog.

EQUANIMITY (ee-kwa-nim-et-tee) patience; calm; evenness of temperament and composure.
Remember: Kindness EQUALS our ANIMOSITY.
Answer: I removed the pile of leaves. Ablation means to remove or take away.

Sep 10

The new paradigm that the earth was round made sales of the old square globes go flat.

PARADIGM (par-ah-dime) pattern; standard; model; thinking the same common belief.
Remember: PARAPHRASE DIMES are a decade.
Question: You eat cookies made by your friend. You say, "These are emetic!" Why does your friend look at you funny?

Sep 11

The goose took a gander at the flower.

GANDER (gan-der) peek; glance; look; looking around at new things.
Remember: Our eyes MEANDER.
Answer: Emetic means causing vomit.

Sep 12

The saqacious cat could do math.

SAGACIOUS (sah-gay-shish) keen; wise;
perceiving and understanding quickly.
Remember: SAGA is SPACIOUS and keen.
Question: We are swimming. I say, "Your tact is
annoying." What will you probably do next?

Sep 13

THE IMPORTUNATE BIRDS
WERE PESKY AND
ANNOYING.

IMPORTUNATE (im-poor-choo-nit) persistent;
annoying and bothering pest.
Remember: pressing at an UNFORTUNATE time.
Answer: Stop touching me. Tact means to touch. It
also means to handle something with great care and
thought.

Sep 14

I KNOW A WAY I CAN COAX,
YOU TO DO STUFF FOR ME,
BRIBE YOU GOOD WITH A COKE,
WHEN YOU ARE THIRSTY.

COAX (cokes) persuade; manipulate; tend;
convincing someone to act by talking.
Remember: COKES to persuade them.
Question: Do you have trepidation about going out in
tepid weather?

Sep 15

Birds are germane to bees
because they both fly.

GERMANE (germ-main) pertinent; akin; relevant;
common bond between two topics.
Remember: GERMS are MAIN related and close.
Answer: No! Tepid means warm. Trepidation means
to have fear.

Sep 16

IRKSOME (erk-sum) pesky; tedious; bothersome; incessantly frustrating.
Remember: JERK is SOME annoyance.
Question: You see a man standing on a dado. He ignores you. Why does he not talk to you?

Sep 17

PERSNICKETY (per-snik-et-tee) picky; fussy; finicky minded and hard to please.
Remember: PURSE our lips when we are PICKY.
Answer: He is a statue. A dado is the pedestal that a statue stands on.

Sep 18

MOLLIFY (mol-lee-fye) placate; pacify; appease; making someone happy by saying kind things.
Remember: MOLE uses LIFTY happy words.
Question: We will dine wherever your caprice takes us. You don't own a car. Where do we go?

Sep 19

REMONSTRATE (re-mon-strayt) plead; fight; disputing an opposing argument.
Remember: DEMONSTRATE against an argument.
Answer: I don't know. Caprice means to change your mind on a whim. We will go where you want to go.

Sep 20

Coffee is the one hedonic thing I enjoy each day.

HEDONIC (he-don-nik) pleasurable; decadent; wanton and full of pleasure.
Remember: HEADY TONIC is fun.
Question: I tell you, "I love your dowdy hat!" Why don't you thank me?

Sep 21

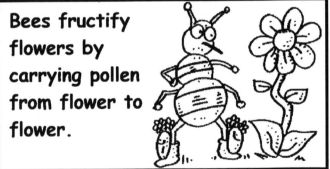

Bees fructify flowers by carrying pollen from flower to flower.

FRUCTIFY (frook-tee-feye) pollinate; fertilize; impregnate to bear fruit by pollination.
Remember: FRUIT MULTIPLIES.
Answer: Dowdy means to be vulgar looking or to be in bad taste. I said, "I love your ugly hat."

Sep 22

The tent was a bit prententious because of the chimney.

PRETENTIOUS (pre-ten-shush) pompous; showy; making it grander to impress people.
Remember: PRETEND TO US.
Question: A bee does not have hoofs. How does a bee, behoove you?

Sep 23

The epilogue ended the book with a happy ending.

EPILOGUE (ep-pee-log) follow-up; postscript; summarizing a book with a conclusion.
Remember: EPIC LOG tells how it ended.
Answer: It makes honey. Behoove means to use or profit from. You benefit when you eat the honey.

The
trophy
was a great
accolade.

ACCOLADE (ak-co-laid) praise; applaud; salute; showing appreciation with an award.
Remember: ACCEPT AID as an award.
Question: You show up on an antedate for a date. How was your date?

His punctilious brushstrokes were great.

PUNCTILIOUS (punk-til-lee-us) precise; correct; strictly doing with care and attention to detail.
Remember: PUNCTUAL for US.
Answer: Not good. Antedate is a date earlier than a given date. You showed up early and your date was not there.

Sep 26

PRESCIENT (pres-shent) predict; visionary; insight; foreseeing events in the future.

Remember: PREDICT and have a SENSE.

Question: You are a veracious and ravenous. You say, "You did not eat the pie." I believe you. Why?

Sep 27

GESTATION (jes-tay-shun) pregnancy; incubation; carrying a baby inside a womb from conception.

Remember: GUEST in the STATION.

Answer: A veracious person tells the truth. Veracious means having the habit of being honest.

ESOTERIC (es-o-ter-rik) private; exclusive; cryptic; secret only understood with confidential knowledge.
Remember: It IS a SECRET.
Question: You go trundling. What do you do with your balls?

CAVALCADE (kav-al-kayd) procession; caravan; parade on horseback or in cars.
Remember: CAVALRY parade goes by.
Answer: You throw them down the lane. Trundling means to bowl.

Sep 30

I had a presage that I would play in the snow today.

PRESAGE (pres-sadge) prophecy; forewarning; boding intuition or foresight.
Remember: PREDICT as a SAGE.
Question: Is your commorancy common or is it fancy?

Oct 1

The new plant food made my flowers burgeon.

BURGEON (bur-gin) prosper; blossom; flourish; blooming at a great rate and growing fast.
Remember: BURSTS for an EON.
Answer: It depends. A commorancy is the place where you live or sleep.

Oct 2

IT'S AN AUSPICIOUS DAY,
FOR YOU CAN SEE,
MONEY CAME MY WAY,
AND I WON THE LOTTERY!

AUSPICIOUS (or-spish-shus) prosperous;
lucky and favoured by fortune or a new beginning.
Remember: AWED fortune is DELICIOUS.
Question: You come home and realize your brazier is
hot. Why are you happy about it?

Oct 3

We had a felicitous time.

FELICITOUS (fel-lis-set-tus) prosperous; jolly;
joyous and pleasant situation.
Remember: DELICIOUS when we are happy.
Answer: A brazier holds hot coal. Your house is nice
and warm. Pronounced: Bray-zure

Oct 4

The bull was a bulwark for the mouse.

BULWARK (bull-wark) protect; guard; fort; fortifying and safeguarding.
Remember: BULL WORKS to protect us.
Question: Your eyes belie where your ball lies. Do I know where your ball is?

Oct 5

It was a mistake to quibble with a cat.

QUIBBLE (kwib-bul) protest; bicker; disagree; verbally fighting about unimportant things.
Remember: QUIZ like a BULL.
Answer: Yes. Your eyes give away where your ball is. Belie means to reveal a secret.

Oct 6

DO YOU READ A GAZETTE,
IT HAS NEWS AND MORE,
IF YOU DON'T YOU MAY REGRET,
NOT KNOWING WHAT WAS BEFORE.

GAZETTE (ga-zet) magazine; newspaper;
publication providing news or a daily paper.
Remember: GAZE at IT.
Question: You don't like germane things. Why don't
you respond when someone greets you?

Oct 7

The officious woman told me what to eat.

OFFICIOUS (oh-fish-ish) pushy; intrusive;
meddling and giving unwanted advice.
Remember: OFFICIAL and VICIOUS.
Answer: Germane means appropriate. You don't like
appropriate things like greeting people.

Oct 8

I CANNOT SOLVE IT,
IT WILL ADDLE ME,
I DON'T HAVE THE WIT,
A PUZZLE IT WILL BE.

ADDLE (ah-del) puzzle; baffle; muddle; confused about an unsolvable problem.
Remember: ADDS up LESS.
Question: Your car has a stalwart engine. Can you drive it or does it stall?

Oct 9

The cat always seemed to what to slake his thirst. We never knew just why.

SLAKE (slayke) quench; refresh; satisfy; quenching thirst with a drink.
Remember: LAKE will stop thirst.
Answer: You can drive it. Stalwart means being strong. Your car has a strong engine.

He was a true bibliophile and he owned a lot of books.

BIBLIOPHILE (bib-lee-oh-file) reader; scholar; intellectual who loves books.
Remember: BIBLE LOVER.
Question: Tonight, I will lock my doors and lucubrate for hours. What am I doing?

A good stick will always hamper a snake.

HAMPER (ham-per) refrain; obstruct; curb; hinder by blocking.
Remember: In a HAMPER and blocked.
Answer: Studying. Lucubrate means to work or study at night.

Oct 12

VESTIGE (ves-tidge) relic; remnant; remains; existing only in pieces of evidence.
Remember: INVESTIGATE the evidence.
Question: A cetacean swims by our boat. Why are we not afraid?

Oct 13

APPEASE (ah-pees) relieve; placate; soothe; creating a feeling of peace and calm.
Remember: APPLAUD when it is EASED.
Answer: A cetacean is a dolphin or a whale. Cetacean means an aquatic mammal having a blowhole.

Oct 14

YOU GIVE UP YOUR
CROWN WHEN YOU
ABDICATE

ABDICATE (ab-dee-kayt) relinquish; step down; resign from a position or job.
Remember: ABANDON being a DICTATOR.
Question: You cogitate loaves of bread. What will you probably do next?

Oct 15

WHEN YOU ABJURE, YOU QUIT YOUR CLUB, BETTER BE SURE, YOU'RE NOT MAKING A FLUB.

ABJURE (ab-jur) repudiate; reject; disavow; abandoning an oath and giving up an allegiance.
Remember: ABDICATE and JERK away.
Answer: Think about something more interesting. Cogitate means to think deeply. Thinking about bread is boring.

Oct 16

There was not a single denizen around.

DENIZEN (den-ne-zen) resident; citizen; occupant; living as a dweller in a habitat.
Remember: CITIZEN dwells in a room.
Question: California is not caliginous. How can that be?

Oct 17

I TAKE A GOOD REPOSE,
AND GET A LOT OF SLEEP.
PAJAMAS ARE MY CLOTHES,
IN CASE I'M COUNTING SHEEP.

REPOSE (re-poze) rest; slumber; rest;
resting in a peaceful position.
Remember: RETURN to a POSE.
Answer: California is bright and sunny. Caliginous means being dark and gloomy.

Oct 18

PARAPHRASE (pa-ra-fraze) restate; recap; reword; rewording to clarify and explain better.
Remember: PARABLE as a new PHRASE.
Question: We play scrabble. You want to quit. I say quitting is an obliquity thing to do. Why do you sit back down and play?

Oct 19

AFFLATUS (ah-flat-tus) revelation; vision; insight; creative impulse.
Remember: INFLATE US with inspiration.
Answer: Obliquity means dishonest or underhanded.

Oct 20

The robot venerated the soda machine.

VENERATE (ven-ah-rayte) reverence; cherish; admiring or holding in the highest regard.
Remember: VENT a good RATE for you.
Question: You get in your car and forgo a road trip. How was your trip?

Oct 21

Carrot cake is the antithesis of a carrot. But we both thought they were delicious.

ANTITHESIS (ant-tith-ee-sis) reverse; counter; contrasting against the exact opposite.
Remember: ANTI THESIS is the opposite.
Answer: You never took it. Forgo means to give up or to not do.

Oct 22

PROPERTIED (prop-per-teed) rich; wealthy;
prosperously owning land and a lot of money.
Remember: Owns PROPERTY.
Question: You abrade the hair on a tiger. What
should you do next?

Oct 23

APROPOS (ap-pro-po) right; good; suitable;
good timing and appropriate actions.
Remember: APPROPRIATE and POSITIVE.
Answer: Run! Abrade means to scrape off or wear
down by rubbing.

COMMODIOUS (kom-mowd-dee-us) Roomy; big; grand spacious place.

Remember: COMMON space for US.

Question: You are a sailboat captain. You yell, "Put up the sails and scuttle ahead!" How fast do you go?

CAPACIOUS (ca-pay-she-us) roomy; large; ample; spaciously big and ample.

Remember: Where we lay our CAP is SPACIOUS.

Answer: You don't. You sink your boat. Scuttle means to sink a ship on purpose.

Oct 26

SKIFF (skif) rowboat; sailboat; dinghy; small tiny boat.
Remember: A small boat SKIPS across the water.
Question: I drink lemonade, but I never drink promenade. Why?

Oct 27

BOISTEROUS (boy-stur-rouse) rowdy; riotous; wildly loud and noisy.
Remember: BOYS STIR and ROUST.
Answer: A promenade is a walkway or a street. It also means a dance or a party.

Oct 28

One rabbit was enough to ensure the perdition of my beautiful garden.

PERDITION (per-dish-shun) ruin; loss; punishment; complete destruction and ruin.
Remember: PERILOUS CONDITION.
Question: You write: "I am a mimick and I will write about spelling." I write back: "You're not good." Why am I right?

Oct 29

A cow stood alone in the agrarian landscape.

AGRARIAN (ah-grair-re-an) rural; peasant; farming; field or large piece of green land.
Remember: GRASS GRAIN covers the countryside.
Answer: Mimick is spelled as mimic.

Oct 30

It took a long time to tame the feral cat but we soon became friends.

FERAL (fer-ral) savage; untamed; undomesticated; wild, untamed and timid animal.

Remember: FUR ALL scared.

Question: You read a book each day. Why is it a quotidian habit?

Oct 31

His erudition was the secret to his selling success.

ERUDITION (ee-ru-dish-shun) scholarship; learning cultured and refined education.

Remember: EDUCATION we learned.

Answer: Quotidian means to do the same thing everyday.

Nov 1

PEDAGOGY (ped-ah-go-gee) schooling; learning; the science or art of teaching.
Remember: Learn from a PEDIA and we are AGOG.
Question: You let out a whelp! We both go running down the street. Why?

Nov 2

HERMETIC (her-met-tik) sealed; tight; shut; isolating from all outside influences.
Remember: HERMIT TIC when hidden.
Answer: A whelp is a puppy. We have to get it.

Nov 3

SEQUESTER (see-kwes-ter) seclude; separate; isolated and hidden from other people.
Remember: SET on a QUEST and stay away.
Question: Is a confabulation always fabulous?

Nov 4

HEDONIST (heed-don-ist) self-indulgent; glutton; wantonly wanting only pleasure.
Remember: HEADY when an ADONIS.
Answer: It depends on the speakers. A confabulation is a conversation or a speech.

Nov 5

She always had a beatific look on her pretty face.

BEATIFIC (be-ah-tif-ick) serene; radiant; blissful; showing great joy.
Remember: BEAUTIFUL and TERRIFIC.
Question: You go fishing. You put a metacarpus on the shoulder of your friend. Why doesn't he mind?

Nov 6

MY HAT MAY BE DOWDY,

BUT I WEAR IT WITH PRIDE,

WHEN IT'S WET AND CLOUDY,

I'M GLAD THAT IT'S WIDE.

DOWDY (dow-dee) shabby; frumpy; drab; lacking style or elegance.
Remember: Say "OW" when it hurts to look at.
Answer: A metacarpus is a hand.

Nov 7

REPROACH (re-proach) shame; discredit; disgrace; finding blame or fault.

Remember: REPEAT our APPROACH.

Question: You ruminate on things while you ruminate a lettuce sandwich. What are you doing?

Nov 8

TRENCHANT (trench-chant) sharp; keen; biting; severely replying in a forceful way.

Remember: ENTRENCH an ANT and it will bite.

Answer: You are thinking while chewing a lettuce sandwich. Ruminate means to think but ruminate also means to chew.

Nov 9

He learned using a thermometer and a light bulb is a great way to malinger.

MALINGER (ma-leen-ger) shirk; loaf; dodge. pretending to be sick to get out of work or school.
Remember: Pretend to be MAL so we can LINGER.
Question: You have vignettes with vinegar. What do you have?

Nov 10

Your behavior is egregious and insulting.

EGREGIOUS (ee-gre-jis) shocking; extreme; glaring, offensive and egregious act.
Remember: OUTRAGEOUS.
Answer: You have short movies and vinegar. Vignette means a short movie. You are enjoying vinegar while watching a movie.

Nov 11

CANNY (cane-nee) shrewd; astute; clever; clever and smart.

Remember: CAN do things.

Question: You are in a boat. You come upon a regale. Instead of a raincoat, you put on a shiny hat. Why?

Nov 12

TACITURN (tas-it-turn) silent; aloof; close-mouthed and not inclined to talking.

Remember: Use TACT until my TURN.

Answer: A regale is a party. You put on a party hat.

Nov 13

RETICENT (ret-tee-sent) silent; shy; hesitant; reluctant to speak.
Remember: RETIRE and SENT you away.
Question: How can a centipede be an antipode to an annelid? Tough question.

Nov 14

GRASPABLE (grasp-ah-bul) simple; obvious; clear; comprehendible and understandable.
Remember: GRASP we are ABLE for it is clear.
Answer: Antipode means opposite of. A centipede has legs. An annelid is a worm and has no legs. They are opposites in that way.

Nov 15

He wore an azure colored shirt covered with little clouds.

AZURE (ah-shore) sky; sapphire; blue;
the colour of blue.
Remember: SHORE sits before blue water.
Question: Your aunt is an antonym to a woman.
What is she to you?

Nov 16

My little house is next to a big edifice.

EDIFICE (ed-ee-face) skyscraper; monument;
large Impressive building.
Remember: EDDY flows up the OFFICE.
Answer: Nothing. The woman is not related to you
and your aunt is. They are antonyms to each other.
Opposites.

I WENT TO FLY A KITE
BUT THE WIND WAS TORPID,
SO IT WOULD NOT TAKE FLIGHT,
NO MATTER WHAT I DID.

TORPID (tore-pid) sluggish; dormant;lazy; motionless and still.

Remember: TORE our PEDS and we cannot move.

Question: Your solution has great efficacy. Do I like it?

He showed great acumen when it came to getting out of work.

ACUMEN (ack-qew-men) smartness; brains; shrewdly able to make quick decisions.

Remember: ACUTE MEN are smart.

Answer: Yes. Your solution is good. Efficacy means being able to produce an effect.

Nov 19

The priggish woman made us eat veggies.

PRIGGISH (prig-esh) smug; vain; stuffy;
annoying person who likes petty rules.
Remember: PIGGISH when we annoy with rules.
Question: You are vociferous. You wear a florid hat.
Why do they throw you out of the library?

Nov 20

We had great sodality in our club.

SODALITY (so-dahl-lit-tee) society; association;
brotherhood of friends or comrades.
Remember: SODA in TOTALITY for all.
Answer: Vociferous means being loud and noisy.
You are too noisy in the library.

UTTER (ud-der) speak; talk; blurt; saying words incoherently.
Remember: MUTTER.
Question: You write: "The automobile license is accepable." Why don't I understand what you wrote?

CELERITY (sel-ler-rit-tee) speed; hurry; haste; quickly moving.
Remember: ACCELERATE when fast.
Answer: The word is spelled "acceptable." I don't know what "accepable" means. Just remember: Accept the table.

Nov 23

PROMENADE (prom-en-nayde) stroll; mall;
boardwalk with a path.
Remember: PROM has LEMONADE to walk to.
Question: Can you use a magnet to lift up a magnate?

Nov 24

FATUOUS (fat-chew-us) stupid; silly; foolish;
not understanding or dull witted.
Remember: Mind is FAT when said to US.
Answer: No. A magnate is an important person or a
celebrity.

RESPLENDENT (re-splend-dant) sublime; glorious; gleaming and shining brilliantly.
Remember: RESPECT a SPLENDID thing.
Question: You drive your car on a long trip. Should you have a gascon with you?

SUCCUMB (suk-come) submit; surrender; yield; making someone quit or admit defeat.
Remember: SUCCESS will COME later.
Answer: No. A braggart is not good company. A gascon is a boaster or someone who is a know-it-all.

SPLENETIC (splen-net-tik) sullen; testy; spiteful;
gloomy sadness.
Remember: SPLENDID until bothered by a TIC.
Question: You have an impressive John Hancock.
What are you good at?

EXTANT (ex-tant) surviving; alive; living;
existing over a long time.
Remember: EX TENT still exists.
Answer: Signing your name! Your John Hancock is
your signature! A common phrase is "Put your John
Hancock here."

Nov 29

INAMORATA (in-nam-or-rat-ta) sweetheart;
mistress and lover.
Remember: IN AMOUR.
Question: Can you outrun a snafu?

Nov 30

ANECDOTE (an-nek-dote) tale; episode; yarn;
telling a short story about an amusing event.
Remember: A NECK makes us DOTE when it talks.
Answer: Yes. A snafu is a mistake. It does not run.

Dec 1

The parable of the story was to be kind to animals.

PARABLE (pa-ra-bil) teaching; tale; legend; teaching a moral lesson with a story.
Remember: PAR for a FABLE.
Question: Do you ever binge on bilge?

Dec 2

He became lachrymose when he could not find his toy.

LACHRYMOSE (lak-ra-mowse) teary; weepy; sorrowful and crying easily.
Remember: CRY MUCH.
Answer: I hope not because bilge is trash.

Dec 3

LOL IS WHAT I SAY,
TO LAUGH OUT LOUD,
IT IS AN FUNNY WAY,
TO MAKE A MIME PROUD.

ARGOT (arg-goht) terminology; lingo; slang; vocabulary only understood by a group.
Remember: What you ARGUE I GOT.
Question: You're lying in a lounge chair. I espy you. Do you stop lounging?

Dec 4

I wonder what my cat thinks about.

COGITATE (kog-gee-tayte) think; ponder; reflect; thinking hard and long about a problem.
Remember: A COG to MEDITATE about.
Answer: No. Espy means to see from a distance. You don't see me.

Dec 5

The mama bird harangued me.

HARANGUE (har-rang) tirade; diatribe; scold; convincing someone by harassing them.
Remember: HARASS until they HANG on words.
Question: You are always coterminous when I come home. I don't mind because I like you. What are you doing?

Dec 6

Tennis will inure you to pain of hitting a ball.

INURE (in-yer) train; toughen; harden; growing accustomed to hardship and pain.
Remember: ENDURE a hardship.
Answer: Being next to me. Coterminous means next to or near.

Dec 7

I closely read the minutia.

MINUTIA (min-noo-sha) trifle; minimal; trivial; small or unimportant details.
Remember: MINIMUM when it is TRIVIAL.
Question: Race car, kayak and toot. Something is very special about these words. The secret is in a mirror. What is the secret?

Dec 8

She wore big pretty baubles around her neck.

BAUBLE (baw-bul) trinket; ornament; trifle; cheap but beautiful jewellery.
Remember: BAW when your jewellery is BULL.
Answer: They are spelled the same way backwards or forwards.

Dec 9

VERACIOUS (ver-ray-shus) truthful; credible; habitual ethical practice of honesty.
Remember: VERIFY truth for we are GRACIOUS.
Question: Your money is efflorescence. Are you happy?

Dec 10

OBLIQUITY (ah-blik-qwit-tee) twist; slant; obscure; unclear and confusing beyond comprehension.
Remember: OBLIQUE when not clear to ME.
Answer: Yes! Efflorescence means to flower or grow.

Dec 11

Gravity is still a truly immutable law.

IMMUTABLE (im-mute-ah-bul) unalterable; permanent and unchangeable absolute.
Remember: MUTE for it is not ABLE to change.
Question: You had a garrulous chat. Did you enjoy it?

Dec 12

The instructions were too ambiguous.

AMBIGUOUS (am-big-you-owse) unclear; vague; uncertain and puzzling because of many meanings.
Remember: I AM too BIG to understand.
Answer: No. Garrulous means talking about boring or trivial things. It was not a good chat.

Dec 13

EVINCE (ee-vinse) uncloak; reveal; prove; proving a thing to be true.
Remember: CONVINCE.
Question: Everyone says your web page is too multifarious. It's not good. What should you do to make it better?

Dec 14

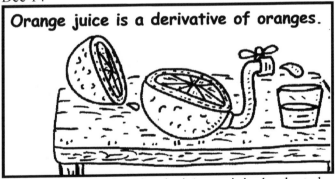

DERIVATIVE (dee-riv-ah-tiv) unoriginal; adapted; copied from a previous secondary version.
Remember: DERIVE the ACTIVE thing.
Answer: Make it simpler! Multifarious means having many different parts.

Dec 15

The rambunctious robot wrecked the room.

RAMBUNCTIOUS (ram-bunk-shus) unruly; rowdy; wildly loud and out of control.

Remember: RAM in a BUNK scares US.

Question: Your sister takes a turn at the cistern. What is she doing?

Dec 16

I TAKE A BATH EACH DAY. IT IS A QUOTIDIAN THING TO DO. HAVE YOU SEEN THE SOAP?

QUOTIDIAN (kwo-tid-ee-an) usual; routine; common repeated daily habit.

Remember: Meeting a QUOTA each DAY.

Answer: Drinking water from a vessel. (Pronounced) sis-turn. A cistern is a tank for holding water or other liquids.

Dec 17

ARRANT (air-rant) utter; total;
completely or entirely absolute.
Remember: ARE RANT for it is total.
Question: I am going to inculcate you. You will like
it. What will I do to you?

Dec 18

DEVOID (dee-voyd) vacant; barren; empty;
bare and lacking.
Remember: THE VOID is vacant.
Answer: It means that I am going to teach you
persistently and earnestly. Inculcate is pronounced:
In-kul-kayt

Dec 19

The little dog had too much hubris.

HUBRIS (you-bris) vanity; pride; arrogance; exaggerated confidence.
Remember: YOU BRISTLE with confidence.
Question: Your house is capacious! What kind of house do you have?

Dec 20

The boy ran with verve and energy.

VERVE (verv) vitality; gusto; vigour; acting with great energy.
Remember: NERVE when we have energy.
Answer: You have a spacious house. It is big and roomy. Remember: Capacious sounds like spacious.

Dec 21

SALUTARY (sal-you-tare-ee) wholesome; healing; nourishing and beneficial to health.

Remember: SALUTE and enjoy the AIRY day.

Question: I see a vestige of a loaf of bread. What do I probably see?

Dec 22

JUDICIOUS (ju-dish-ish) wise; Sober; Sane; reasonable and fair.

Remember: A good JUDGE.

Answer: Crumbs. A vestige is evidence that something existed and no longer exists.

Dec 23

HALLOO (hal-lew) yell; cry; scream;
loud hollering or shouting.
Remember: HAIL YOU to look.
Question: You are reading my paraphrase right now.
What are you reading?

Dec 24

CAPITULATE (kah-pit-chew-layte) yield; quit;
surrendering and relenting to a foe.
Remember: CAPITAL too LATE to win.
Answer: You are reading a sentence written in a
clearer way. Paraphrase means to reword something
to clarify it.

Dec 25

ARDENT (ar-dent) zealous; eager; passionate; fan or enthusiastic supporter.
Remember: ARE making a DENT for they are eager.
Question: Why is an ant, procreant?

Dec 26

EBULLIENCE (ee-bul-yents) zest; elation; overflowing with exuberance and happiness.
Remember: BULLHORN breaks the SILENCE.
Answer: An ant procreates well. They make more ants quickly.

Dec 27

OOMPH (oomf) zing; dash; pep;
energy and zest.
Remember: OHM is a measure of energy.
Question: You make bathos in a bathtub. What did
you do?

Dec 28

SUPERFLUOUS (soo-pa-flew-us) unneeded;
excessively large amount.
Remember: SUPER FLUID.
Answer: You made a crude joke. Bathos is switching
from talking in a high-class way to a low-class way.

Dec 29

I expiate my guilt for eating the cookies.

EXPIATE (ex-pee-ate) atone; amend; absolve; seeking forgiveness for a guilty action.
Remember: EX PAST so I apologize.
Question: I bring a conundrum. The band stops playing and listens to me. Why does the band look confused?

Dec 30

The zeitgeist of the time was wearing flowered hats.

ZEITGEIST (zite-guyst) attitude; outlook; characteristics representing the spirit of a time.
Remember: SITE GHOST.
Answer: A conundrum is a riddle. It makes no music. The band is puzzled by my riddle.

He will always extol his cat.
~ The End

EXTOL

(ex-toll) bless; glorify; laud;
praising a person or a thing.
Remember: EXCELLENT TOLL of you.

38827804R00106

Made in the USA
Middletown, DE
28 December 2016